1

MW01040988

# WORKBOOK

## Self Heal By Design- The Role Of Micro-Organisms For Health by Barbara O'Neill

**Thank you!**

thank you for choosing the workbook "Self Heal By Design- The Role Of Micro-Organisms For Health Workbook". These resources will help you apply the teachings and principles of the book to live a life that is both fulfilling and healthy.

The workbook includes additional exercises, prompts, and resources to help you further explore the topics covered in the book. You will also find a section on troubleshooting common problems and a section on resources for further learning.

Your feedback is important to me, and it would be greatly appreciated if you could take a few minutes to leave a review on Amazon. Your review will help other customers decide whether or not to purchase these products, and it will also help me to improve my products and services.

If you have any questions or comments, please don't hesitate to reach out. I am always happy to hear from my customers and to help them in any way that I can.

Thank you for your time and consideration.

3

## Disclaimer

This workbook is a companion to the book Self Heal By Design- The Role Of Micro-Organisms For Health by Barbara O'Neill. It is not intended to replace the original book, but rather to provide additional exercises and resources to help you apply the teachings of the book to your own life.

The author of this workbook encourages you to purchase the original book and read it. The original book provides a comprehensive overview of the Self Heal By Design philosophy, while this workbook provides a more hands-on approach to help you implement the philosophy in your own life.

This workbook is not affiliated with the authors of the original book, and it does not reflect their opinions or views. The author of this workbook is solely responsible for the content of this workbook.

The reader is encouraged to use their own judgment and discretion when working through the exercises in this workbook. The author of this workbook does not endorse any particular approach to improving gut health and overall well-being, and the reader is responsible for their own results.

This workbook is not a substitute for professional medical advice. If you are seeking medical advice, please consult with a qualified medical professional.

# Table of Contents

# **<u>CHAPTER 1: Sickness Is No Accident: The Body Has A Plan</u>**

Chapter 1 of the book "Self Heal by Design" explores the concept that sickness is not an accident, but rather a response by the body to an imbalance or dysfunction. The authors emphasize the idea that the body has a natural ability to heal itself if provided with the right conditions. They introduce the concept of self-healing and stress the importance of understanding the body's natural healing mechanisms.

The chapter begins by discussing the link between fungus and cancer. The authors highlight the work of researchers such as Professor A.V Constantine, Doug Kaufmann, and Dr Tullio Simoncini, who have all demonstrated the connection between fungus and disease, including cancer. They explain that fungi and their waste products, called mycotoxins, can cause major diseases in humans. Additionally, the authors mention the use of sodium bicarbonate as a treatment for cancer, as it can create an alkaline environment that kills cancer cells.

The authors also emphasize the role of emotional health, proper hydration, and diet in cancer treatment. They mention the research of Dr T. Colin Campbell, who found that high levels of animal protein can promote cancer growth, while low levels of protein or plant-based protein can reduce tumor growth. They also discuss the devastating effects of chemotherapy on the body and the need for alternative approaches to cancer treatment.

Moving on, the chapter delves into the concept that sickness is the body's way of communicating an underlying issue that needs to be addressed. It highlights the body's natural ability to heal itself and the importance of understanding the body's plan for optimal health. The authors stress the role of the immune system in maintaining health and fighting off illness. They explain that the immune system is designed to protect the body from harmful pathogens and maintain a state of balance, or homeostasis. However, when the body is exposed to stress, toxins, or other imbalances, the immune system can become compromised and lead to illness.

The chapter concludes by emphasizing the importance of taking responsibility for one's own health and well-being. It encourages readers to explore alternative approaches to healing and to seek out natural remedies and therapies that support the body's innate healing abilities. The authors also introduce the concept of the body's pH balance and the impact of acidity and alkalinity on overall health. They stress the need to make conscious choices that support the body's natural healing processes.

Overall, Chapter 1 sets the stage for the rest of the book by introducing the concept of self-healing and emphasizing the importance of understanding the body's natural healing mechanisms. It explores the link between fungus and cancer, discusses the role of emotional health, hydration, and diet in cancer treatment, and highlights the importance of the immune system in maintaining health. The chapter concludes by encouraging readers to take responsibility for their own health and make conscious choices to support the body's natural healing abilities.

## Key Lessons

1. Sickness is not an accident, but rather the body's response to an imbalance or dysfunction.

2. The body has a natural plan for healing and maintaining health.

3. It is important to understand and support the body's natural healing abilities.

4. Take responsibility for one's own health and understand the underlying causes of illness.

5. Listen to the body and pay attention to any signs or symptoms that may indicate an imbalance.

6. Stress can disrupt the body's natural healing processes and lead to a weakened immune system.

7. Manage stress levels to support the body's healing abilities.

8. The immune system plays a crucial role in fighting off illness and maintaining health.

9. Support the immune system through proper nutrition, lifestyle habits, and stress management.

10. The mind-body connection is important in the healing process, with positive thoughts and emotions supporting healing and negative thoughts and stress hindering it.

11. Take an active role in one's own healing journey and utilize practical tips and strategies for achieving optimal health.

## Reflection Questions

1. How can understanding the body's natural healing mechanisms help us prevent and address sickness?

-----------------------------------------------------------------

-----------------------------------------------------------------

-----------------------------------------------------------------

-----------------------------------------------------------------

-----------------------------------------------------------------

-----------------------------------------------------------------

-----------------------------------------------------------------

-------------------------------------------------------------------

-------------------------------------------------------------------

-------------------------------------------------------------------

-------------------------------------------------------------------

-------------------------------------------------------------------

-------------------------------------------------------------------

-------------------------------------------------------------------

2. What lifestyle habits can we adopt to support the body's plan for healing and maintain optimal health?

-------------------------------------------------------------------

-------------------------------------------------------------------

-------------------------------------------------------------------

-------------------------------------------------------------------

------------------------------------------------

------------------------------------------------

------------------------------------------------

------------------------------------------------

------------------------------------------------

------------------------------------------------

------------------------------------------------

------------------------------------------------

------------------------------------------------

------------------------------------------------

------------------------------------------------

3. How can we effectively detoxify and eliminate toxins from our bodies to support overall health?

## Action Prompts

1. Reflect on your own beliefs about the body's ability to heal itself.

2. Consider any personal experiences or encounters that have shaped your views on natural health and prevention of illness.

3. Explore your motivations for wanting to learn more about health and wellness.

4. Research different approaches to healthcare, such as naturopathy and nutrition, and their potential benefits.

5. Evaluate the role of diet and lifestyle in maintaining optimal health.

6. Reflect on any experiences or knowledge you have regarding the body's self-healing mechanisms.

7. Consider the impact of illness on your own life or the lives of those close to you.

8. Reflect on the importance of education and spreading correct health principles to others.

9. Consider the potential benefits of incorporating natural health practices into your own life.

10. Reflect on the role of personal experiences and journeys in shaping our beliefs and passions.

# CHAPTER 2: Historical Moments: What Does The Past Tell Us?

Chapter 2 of the book "Self Heal by Design" delves into the historical moments that shed light on the connection between fungus and disease. The chapter begins by examining biblical references to leprosy, which are now believed to refer to mildew or fungal infections. This highlights the long-standing knowledge that fungus has been a cause of disease in humans for centuries.

The chapter then introduces the work of various scientists and researchers who have studied the role of fungus in disease. Florence Nightingale, renowned for her nursing work during the Crimean War, believed that disease was a reparative process and that microorganisms in the body played a role in this process. Professors Antoine Bechamp and Gunther Enderlein also observed the pleomorphic nature of microorganisms, meaning they can change form depending on the environment.

Dr. Tullio Simoncini's research on the link between fungus and cancer is also mentioned. Simoncini has found that sodium bicarbonate can be used as a treatment for cancer, as it creates an alkaline environment that is toxic to fungus. Additionally, other researchers like Dr. T. Colin Campbell have discovered a connection between high animal protein consumption and cancer, suggesting that plant-based diets may offer protection against cancer.

Overall, the chapter presents evidence from various sources that support the idea of fungus playing a significant role in human disease, including cancer. By exploring historical moments and the research of scientists, the chapter establishes a foundation for understanding the link between fungus and disease.

In addition to discussing the link between fungus and disease, the chapter also explores the broader theme of historical moments and their significance. It highlights the importance of learning from the past and using that knowledge to improve the present and future. The chapter emphasizes that history repeats itself and that understanding past events can lead to better decision-making in our own lives.

Examples of historical moments, such as the discovery of penicillin and the development of the atomic bomb, are provided to illustrate the impact that these events have had on society. The chapter emphasizes the need to understand the context in which these events occurred and the lessons that can be learned from them.

The chapter concludes by emphasizing the individual's responsibility for their own health and well-being. It encourages readers to learn from both the mistakes and successes of the past and to make informed choices about their own health and lifestyle.

Overall, Chapter 2 of "Self Heal by Design" provides a detailed exploration of historical moments and their significance in understanding the link between fungus and disease. It underscores the importance of learning from the past and using that knowledge to make informed decisions in the present and future.

## Key Lessons

The key lessons from Chapter 2 of the book "Self Heal by Design" are:

1. The link between disease and fungus: The chapter explores historical moments that reveal the connection between disease and fungal infections. It discusses biblical references to leprosy, which is now understood to be a form of fungal infection. This highlights the importance of recognizing the role of fungus in human disease.

2. Pleomorphism vs. monomorphism: The concept of pleomorphism, which is the ability of microorganisms to change form depending on the environment, challenges the traditional view of monomorphism, which states that microorganisms have a fixed form. This challenges the traditional understanding of disease and highlights the need to consider the adaptability of microorganisms.

3. Importance of understanding the body's internal environment: The chapter mentions various scientists and researchers who recognized the importance of understanding the body's internal environment and the role of microorganisms in disease. This emphasizes the need to consider lifestyle factors and the impact they have on fungal growth and overall health.

4. Mycotoxins and their impact on health: The presence of mycotoxins, toxic waste products produced by fungi, is discussed in the chapter. It provides examples of specific mycotoxins and the diseases they can cause, such as aflatoxin and liver cancer. This highlights the importance of being aware of potential sources of mycotoxin exposure and their impact on health.

5. Learning from history: The chapter emphasizes the importance of understanding the past in order to gain insight and knowledge for the present and future. It encourages readers to learn from

historical moments, both successes and mistakes, to make informed decisions in their own lives. By studying historical moments, readers can gain a deeper understanding of human nature, societal patterns, and the consequences of certain actions.

Overall, Chapter 2 of "Self Heal by Design" teaches us the importance of recognizing the role of fungus in disease, considering the adaptability of microorganisms, understanding the body's internal environment, being aware of mycotoxins and their impact on health, and learning from history to make informed decisions.

## Reflection Questions

1. How have historical moments discussed in Chapter 2 deepened my understanding of the link between fungus and disease?

-------------------------------------------------------------------

-------------------------------------------------------------------

-------------------------------------------------------------------

-------------------------------------------------------------------

-------------------------------------------------------------------

------------------------------------------------------

------------------------------------------------------

------------------------------------------------------

------------------------------------------------------

------------------------------------------------------

------------------------------------------------------

------------------------------------------------------

------------------------------------------------------

------------------------------------------------------

2. In what ways have the historical moments mentioned in Chapter 2 shaped my perspective on the importance of studying history?

------------------------------------------------------

------------------------------------------------------

3. What insights can I gain from the historical moments discussed in Chapter 2 that can help me make more informed decisions regarding my health and well-being?

-------------------------------------------------------------------

-------------------------------------------------------------------

-------------------------------------------------------------------

-------------------------------------------------------------------

-------------------------------------------------------------------

-------------------------------------------------------------------

-------------------------------------------------------------------

-------------------------------------------------------------------

-------------------------------------------------------------------

-------------------------------------------------------------------

-------------------------------------------------------------------

-------------------------------------------------------------------

---------------------------------------------------------------

---------------------------------------------------------------

4. How can I actively apply the lessons learned from the historical moments in Chapter 2 to my own life and contribute to the understanding and prevention of human diseases related to fungus?

---------------------------------------------------------------

---------------------------------------------------------------

---------------------------------------------------------------

---------------------------------------------------------------

---------------------------------------------------------------

---------------------------------------------------------------

---------------------------------------------------------------

---------------------------------------------------------------

---------------------------------------------------------------

------------------------------------------------

------------------------------------------------

------------------------------------------------

------------------------------------------------

------------------------------------------------

------------------------------------------------

## Action Prompts

1. Reflect on biblical verses that describe the cycle of life and the return to dust.

2. Research the role of microorganisms, such as bacteria, fungi, and yeast, in breaking down dead matter.

3. Explore the importance of understanding the role of microorganisms in maintaining a healthy body.

4. Consider the historical moments that highlight the link between the human body and the cycle of life.

5. Discuss the significance of the concept of microorganisms in relation to the human body.

6. Analyze the impact of historical events on our understanding of the human body and its connection to the cycle of life.

# CHAPTER 3 Familiarising With A Fungus Feast

Chapter 3 of the book "Self Heal by Design" is titled "Familiarising With A Fungus Feast." This chapter delves into the role of fungi in human disease and provides detailed information on the types of foods that promote the growth of fungus in the body.

The chapter begins by explaining that fungi are living microorganisms that are distinct from both plants and animals. They require food to survive, with their favorite food being sugar in all its forms, including refined sugar, honey, maple syrup, and the sugar found in fruits. The chapter also highlights certain foods that are more susceptible to mold growth, such as alcoholic beverages, yeast bread, peanuts, cooked rice, and aged cheeses. These foods can contribute to fungal overgrowth in the body.

Moving on, the chapter explores the concept of fungal evolution and invasion in the human body. It explains that when there is cell damage in the body, microorganisms like bacteria, fungi, and yeast can evolve into different forms to aid in the repair process. However, if the body's internal environment is imbalanced, these microorganisms can multiply and cause disease. The chapter also discusses the various ways in which mold and fungus can enter the

25

body, including ingestion of moldy food, inhalation of mold spores, skin contact with mold, and even sexual transmission.

To support the idea that fungus plays a significant role in human disease, the author provides examples of researchers and scientists who have studied the fungal link to disease. These include Florence Nightingale, Antoine Bechamp, and Royal Raymond Rife, who have observed the pleomorphic nature of microorganisms, meaning they can change form depending on the conditions in the body. The chapter also mentions the work of Dr. Tullio Simoncini, who has found a link between fungus and cancer and has had success in treating cancer with sodium bicarbonate.

The chapter then focuses on practical guidance for combating fungal infections through dietary modifications. It suggests eliminating sugar and yeast from the diet to starve the fungus, as these are the primary sources of nourishment for fungi. On the other hand, certain foods like legumes, vegetables, grains, and fruits are mentioned to contain antifungal properties and can help in combating fungus. Additionally, the chapter emphasizes the importance of maintaining a proper pH balance in the body, as fungus thrives in an acidic environment. It recommends incorporating alkaline-forming foods, such as green vegetables and grasses, into the diet to create a more alkaline environment that is unfavorable for fungus growth.

In summary, Chapter 3 of "Self Heal by Design" provides a comprehensive exploration of the role of fungus in human disease. It highlights the types of foods that promote fungal overgrowth and provides guidance on modifying the diet to prevent and combat fungal infections. The chapter also presents historical examples and scientific research that support the idea of fungus playing a significant role in disease. Overall, it emphasizes the importance of maintaining a balanced internal environment and avoiding foods that promote fungal growth.

## Key Lessons

1. Fungus thrives on sugar and its favorite food is sugar in all its forms, including refined sugar, honey, maple syrup, and the sugar found in fruits. Consuming these foods encourages fungal growth.

2. Fungus can enter the human body through ingestion of moldy food or antibiotics, inhalation of mold spores, penetration through the skin, and sexual transmission.

3. Fungal spores can remain dormant until they find a suitable environment with a good food supply, and if conditions are right, they can multiply and cause disease.

4. Researchers such as Professor A.V Constantine, Dr. Tullio Simoncini, and Dr. Robert Young have found evidence linking fungus to cancer and other diseases.

5. Maintaining an alkaline pH balance in the body is important to prevent the growth and spread of fungus, as fungus thrives in an

acidic environment. Alkaline-forming foods and green vegetables can help maintain a healthy pH balance.

6. Lifestyle habits such as proper breathing, exercise, and exposure to sunlight can also impact the body's ability to prevent fungal overgrowth.

## Reflection Questions

1. How can I incorporate more mushrooms into my diet to benefit from their nutritional value and immune-boosting properties?

------------------------------------------------------------

------------------------------------------------------------

------------------------------------------------------------

------------------------------------------------------------

------------------------------------------------------------

------------------------------------------------------------

------------------------------------------------------------

------------------------------------------------------------

------------------------------------------------------------

------------------------------------------------------------

------------------------------------------------------------

------------------------------------------------------------

------------------------------------------------------------

------------------------------------------------------------

------------------------------------------------------------

2. What are some creative and delicious recipes that I can try using mushrooms as the main ingredient?

------------------------------------------------------------

------------------------------------------------------------

------------------------------------------------------------

------------------------------------------------------------

------------------------------------------------------------

----------------------------------------------------------------

----------------------------------------------------------------

----------------------------------------------------------------

----------------------------------------------------------------

----------------------------------------------------------------

----------------------------------------------------------------

----------------------------------------------------------------

----------------------------------------------------------------

----------------------------------------------------------------

3. How can I ensure that the mushrooms I consume are safe and free from any potential contaminants or toxins?

----------------------------------------------------------------

----------------------------------------------------------------

4. What are some other types of fungi that I can explore and experiment with in my cooking to expand my culinary repertoire?

------------------------------------------------------------

------------------------------------------------------------

------------------------------------------------------------

------------------------------------------------------------

------------------------------------------------------------

------------------------------------------------------------

------------------------------------------------------------

------------------------------------------------------------

------------------------------------------------------------

------------------------------------------------------------

------------------------------------------------------------

------------------------------------------------------------

-----------------------------------------------------------------------

-----------------------------------------------------------------------

## Action Prompts

1. Try incorporating mushrooms into your diet by adding them to your favorite dishes.

2. Experiment with different types of mushrooms to discover new flavors and textures.

3. Follow the provided recipe to create a delicious mushroom-based dish.

4. Learn about the benefits of consuming mushrooms and how they can contribute to a healthy diet.

5. Consider the different ways fungus can enter the body and take steps to prevent its growth.

6. Explore the link between fungus and disease, including the potential for certain mycotoxins to cause cancer.

7. Understand the importance of maintaining an alkaline pH balance in the body to prevent the growth of fungus and yeast.

8. Discover the effects of different foods on the growth of fungus and adjust your diet accordingly.

9. Incorporate alkaline-forming foods into your meals to maintain a healthy pH balance.

10. Consider the lifestyle habits that can contribute to a healthy pH balance, such as oxygen, sunshine, rest, and mental health.

# CHAPTER 4 Mycology: The Study Of Fungi

Chapter 4 of the book "Self Heal by Design" is titled "Mycology: The Study of Fungi." This chapter provides a comprehensive overview of fungi and their impact on human health. It begins by explaining that fungi are living microorganisms that are distinct from both plants and animals. They require food to survive, with sugar being their preferred source of nutrition.

The chapter goes on to discuss the various ways in which fungi can enter the human body, including ingestion, inhalation, skin contact, and sexual transmission. It highlights the importance of understanding the role of fungi in disease and the need to address lifestyle habits that promote fungal growth, such as consuming high amounts of sugar and exposure to toxic chemicals.

The author supports their claims with evidence from various researchers and scientists. For example, Florence Nightingale believed that disease is a reparative process and an effort of nature to remedy poisoning or decay. Professor Antoine Bechamp observed that microorganisms in the body can change their form depending on the environment and play a role in the breakdown and repair of cells. Dr. Tullio Simoncini and Dr. Robert Young have also found a connection between fungi and cancer.

The chapter also explores the different types of fungi, their characteristics, and their role in causing diseases. It explains that fungi are diverse organisms that can be found in various environments, including soil, water, and air. They can grow on plants, animals, and humans, leading to infections and diseases of varying severity.

Furthermore, the chapter emphasizes the importance of understanding the different types of fungi and their characteristics in order to effectively treat and prevent fungal infections. It highlights the need for proper hygiene, cleanliness, and a healthy immune system to prevent fungal infections.

In addition, the chapter discusses the use of antifungal treatments, such as sodium bicarbonate, in combating fungal infections. It suggests that addressing lifestyle habits that promote fungal growth and utilizing appropriate treatments can help in addressing fungal overgrowth in the body.

Overall, Chapter 4 of "Self Heal by Design" provides a detailed exploration of mycology, the study of fungi, and its relevance to human health. It presents evidence and insights into the link between fungi and disease, particularly cancer, and emphasizes the importance of understanding and addressing fungal overgrowth in the body.

## Key Lessons

1. Mycology, the study of fungi, began with the discovery of aflatoxin in the early 1960s.

2. Fungal diseases have been known since biblical times.

3. Fungi can cause various health issues if the environment is right for their growth.

4. Fungi can travel through body fluids and affect different parts of the body.

5. Excess estrogen and sugar can trigger fungal growth.

6. Nightshade vegetables like tomatoes and potatoes can contribute to inflammation in the body.

7. Maintaining a proper pH balance in the body is important for preventing fungal diseases.

8. A diet consisting of 80% alkaline-forming foods and 20% acid-forming foods is recommended.

9. Various lifestyle habits, such as oxygen, sunshine, temperance, rest, exercise, water, salt, and mental health, can impact the body's pH balance and overall health.

10. Understanding fungi and maintaining a healthy lifestyle are key to preventing fungal diseases and maintaining optimal health.

## Reflection Questions

1. How does the study of fungi contribute to our understanding of the natural world?

-------------------------------------------------------------------

-------------------------------------------------------------------

-------------------------------------------------------------------

-------------------------------------------------------------------

-------------------------------------------------------------------

-------------------------------------------------------------------

-------------------------------------------------------------------

-------------------------------------------------------------------

-------------------------------------------------------------------

-------------------------------------------------------------------

------------------------------------------------

------------------------------------------------

------------------------------------------------

------------------------------------------------

2. In what ways can fungi be beneficial to human health and well-being?

------------------------------------------------

------------------------------------------------

------------------------------------------------

------------------------------------------------

------------------------------------------------

------------------------------------------------

------------------------------------------------

------------------------------------------------

------------------------------------------------

------------------------------------------------

------------------------------------------------

------------------------------------------------

------------------------------------------------

------------------------------------------------

3. What are some examples of diseases caused by fungi and how can they be prevented or treated?

------------------------------------------------

------------------------------------------------

------------------------------------------------

------------------------------------------------

------------------------------------------------

------------------------------------------------

------------------------------------------------

------------------------------------------------

------------------------------------------------

------------------------------------------------

------------------------------------------------

------------------------------------------------

------------------------------------------------

------------------------------------------------

------------------------------------------------

4. How can the knowledge of mycology be applied in various industries, such as agriculture and pharmaceuticals?

## Action Prompts

1. Research and identify the different types of mycotoxins found in foods.

2. Investigate the role of pleomorphism in bacteria and fungi.

3. Explore the research linking fungi to cancer and the proposed treatments and dietary changes.

4. Examine the importance of maintaining an alkaline pH balance in the body and its effect on fungal growth.

5. Create a list of acid-forming and alkaline-forming foods and develop a meal plan that is 80% alkaline-forming foods.

6. Investigate the effects of breastfeeding and consuming figs on fungal growth on the skin.

7. Explore the impact of nightshade vegetables on inflammation in the body and the potential anti-inflammatory effects of cooked tomatoes.

8. Develop recipes using legumes such as black-eyed peas, red lentils, and chickpeas.

# **CHAPTER 5 Presenting The Evidence, History Of Fungus: The Role Fungus Plays In Human Disease**

Chapter 5 of the book "Self Heal by Design" is titled "Presenting The Evidence, History Of Fungus: The Role Fungus Plays In Human Disease." This chapter provides a comprehensive overview of the link between fungus and human disease, with a particular focus on cancer.

The chapter begins by highlighting the work of various researchers and scientists who have contributed to the understanding of the fungal link in disease over the past century. It mentions the research of Professor A.V Constantine, Doug Kaufmann, Dr Tullio Simoncini, and Dr T. Colin Campbell, among others. These researchers have provided evidence and conducted studies that support the role of fungi and their biological metabolites, mycotoxins, in causing degenerative and cancerous diseases.

The chapter explains how fungi can mutate and change their genetic structure, making them resistant to antifungal therapies. This highlights the importance of addressing fungal infections effectively in order to prevent and treat cancer. One treatment method discussed in the chapter is the use of sodium bicarbonate, which can eliminate the organic material that fungi use for nourishment.

Another key point emphasized in the chapter is the importance of maintaining a low-protein diet, particularly animal protein. High levels of animal protein have been linked to cancer growth, and the chapter cites research studies that have shown the protective effect of low-protein diets or plant protein in reducing tumor growth.

Throughout the chapter, the book presents compelling evidence supporting the fungal link in cancer and other diseases. It discusses the historical presence of fungal infections in ancient civilizations and explains how fungus can enter the body through various means and colonize different parts, leading to infections and health issues.

The chapter concludes by discussing the significance of maintaining an alkaline balance in the body to prevent the growth of fungus. It emphasizes the need to address the root causes of fungal infections and provides information on how to starve and kill the fungus, as well as restore the balance of beneficial microbes in the body.

Overall, Chapter 5 of "Self Heal by Design" provides a detailed and informative exploration of the role of fungus in human disease, particularly cancer. It presents evidence, historical context, and practical strategies for preventing and treating fungal infections to improve overall health.

## Key Lessons

1. Fungus has been linked to various health conditions, including cancer. The chapter presents historical evidence and research that supports this link.

2. Fungi and their waste products, called mycotoxins, can cause degenerative and cancerous diseases in humans. Professor A.V Constantine's research demonstrates this relationship.

3. Dr Tullio Simoncini's book "Cancer is a Fungus" explores the use of sodium bicarbonate as a treatment for cancer, suggesting that fungi, particularly Candida, play a significant role in cancer development and progression.

4. Dr T. Colin Campbell's research found that high levels of animal protein, particularly from meat and dairy products, are associated with an increased risk of cancer. In contrast, low levels of protein from plant sources have a protective effect against cancer.

5. Addressing fungal infections and reducing protein consumption, especially from animal sources, may be beneficial in preventing and treating cancer.

6. Fungus can manifest in different forms, such as candida overgrowth, and can lead to symptoms like skin rashes, digestive problems, and fatigue.

7. Understanding the triggers and factors that contribute to fungal overgrowth is important. Hormonal changes, such as the release of estrogen during menstruation, and the consumption of certain foods, like sugar and figs, can stimulate the growth of fungus.

8. Maintaining a balanced pH balance in the body is crucial to prevent fungal growth.

## Reflection Questions

1. How has the historical evidence of fungus playing a role in human disease shaped our understanding of fungal infections today?

-----------------------------------------------------------------

-----------------------------------------------------------------

46

----------------------------------------------------------

----------------------------------------------------------

----------------------------------------------------------

----------------------------------------------------------

----------------------------------------------------------

----------------------------------------------------------

----------------------------------------------------------

----------------------------------------------------------

----------------------------------------------------------

----------------------------------------------------------

----------------------------------------------------------

----------------------------------------------------------

2. What are some of the key advancements in medical knowledge and technology that have contributed to our understanding of fungal infections?

-----------------------------------------------------------

-----------------------------------------------------------

-----------------------------------------------------------

-----------------------------------------------------------

-----------------------------------------------------------

-----------------------------------------------------------

-----------------------------------------------------------

-----------------------------------------------------------

-----------------------------------------------------------

-----------------------------------------------------------

-----------------------------------------------------------

-----------------------------------------------------------

----------------------------------------------------------------

----------------------------------------------------------------

3. How do common fungal infections, such as athlete's foot and ringworm, impact human health and what are the potential complications they can cause?

----------------------------------------------------------------

----------------------------------------------------------------

----------------------------------------------------------------

----------------------------------------------------------------

----------------------------------------------------------------

----------------------------------------------------------------

----------------------------------------------------------------

----------------------------------------------------------------

----------------------------------------------------------------

------------------------------------------------

------------------------------------------------

------------------------------------------------

------------------------------------------------

------------------------------------------------

------------------------------------------------

4. What mechanisms have been identified to explain the link between fungal infections and chronic health conditions like asthma, allergies, and autoimmune diseases?

------------------------------------------------

------------------------------------------------

------------------------------------------------

------------------------------------------------

------------------------------------------------

------------------------------------------------

----------------------------------------

----------------------------------------

----------------------------------------

----------------------------------------

----------------------------------------

----------------------------------------

----------------------------------------

----------------------------------------

----------------------------------------

## Action Prompts

1. Discuss the historical perspective of fungus and its impact on human health.

2. Explain the evidence supporting the role of fungus in causing human diseases.

3. Describe the various diseases that are associated with fungal infections.

4. Explore the ways in which fungus can enter the human body and cause infections.

5. Discuss the challenges in diagnosing and treating fungal infections.

6. Explain the potential complications and long-term effects of untreated fungal infections.

7. Provide examples of specific fungal infections and their impact on human health.

# CHAPTER 6 The Link Between Fungus And Cancer

Chapter 6 of the book "Self Heal by Design" delves into the fascinating link between fungus and cancer. The chapter presents a comprehensive exploration of the research and findings of various scientists and doctors who have studied the relationship between fungus and disease, particularly cancer.

One of the key researchers mentioned in the chapter is Professor A.V Constantine, who has written books showcasing the connection between fungi and diseases, including cancer. Constantine's research demonstrates that fungi and their waste products, known as mycotoxins, play a significant role in the development of degenerative and cancerous diseases in humans.

Another prominent researcher discussed in the chapter is Doug Kaufmann, who has written extensively on the fungal link to various diseases. Kaufmann's book "The Germ That Causes Cancer" delves into the history of medicine and reveals that the connection between fungus and cancer has been known for over a century.

Dr Tullio Simoncini, a medical doctor and surgeon, is also highlighted in the chapter. Simoncini's book "Cancer is a Fungus" presents compelling evidence supporting the idea that candida, a type of fungus, is the root cause of cancer. He has achieved success in treating cancer by using sodium bicarbonate, which creates an alkaline environment toxic to fungus.

Additionally, the chapter explores the research of Dr T. Colin Campbell, who conducted studies on the relationship between protein consumption and cancer. Campbell's research found that high levels of animal protein were associated with an increased risk of cancer, while low levels of animal protein or higher levels of plant protein were protective against cancer.

Overall, the chapter presents a wealth of evidence and research supporting the notion that fungus plays a significant role in the development of cancer. It emphasizes the importance of addressing fungal infections and maintaining a healthy diet to prevent and treat cancer. The chapter also questions the effectiveness of traditional cancer treatments such as chemotherapy, radiotherapy, and surgery, arguing that they do not address the root causes of cancer and can be harmful to the body. Instead, the chapter suggests exploring alternative treatments that work with the body's natural healing mechanisms.

**Key Lessons**

1. Fungus and cancer have a strong connection: The chapter highlights the research and evidence suggesting that fungus plays a role in the development and progression of cancer.

2. Maintaining a balanced pH level is crucial: The chapter emphasizes the importance of maintaining a balanced pH level in the body to prevent the growth of fungus and reduce the risk of cancer. An acidic environment can promote the growth of fungus and increase the risk of cancer.

3. Lifestyle habits affect the acid/alkaline balance: The chapter discusses various lifestyle habits that can affect the acid/alkaline balance in the body, such as proper breathing, good posture, exercise, fresh air, exposure to sunlight, and mental health.

4. Diet plays a significant role: The chapter provides recommendations for a balanced diet that includes 80% alkaline-forming foods and 20% acid-forming foods. It suggests avoiding or reducing the consumption of sugar, alcohol, caffeine, meat, and dairy products, while increasing the intake of vegetables and other alkaline-forming foods.

5. Alternative treatments and natural healing mechanisms may be more effective: The chapter argues that chemotherapy and other

conventional cancer treatments do not address the root causes of cancer and can be harmful to the body. It suggests that alternative treatments and a focus on the body's natural healing mechanisms may be more effective in treating cancer.

## Reflection Questions

1. How does the presence of fungus in the body contribute to the development and progression of cancer?

----------------------------------------------------------------

----------------------------------------------------------------

----------------------------------------------------------------

----------------------------------------------------------------

----------------------------------------------------------------

----------------------------------------------------------------

----------------------------------------------------------------

----------------------------------------------------------------

----------------------------------------------------------------

-------------------------------------------------------------

-------------------------------------------------------------

-------------------------------------------------------------

-------------------------------------------------------------

-------------------------------------------------------------

-------------------------------------------------------------

2. What are some lifestyle habits and dietary changes that can help maintain a balanced pH level in the body and prevent the growth of fungus and cancer cells?

-------------------------------------------------------------

-------------------------------------------------------------

-------------------------------------------------------------

-------------------------------------------------------------

-------------------------------------------------------------

-------------------------------------------------------------

---------------------------------------------------------------

---------------------------------------------------------------

---------------------------------------------------------------

---------------------------------------------------------------

---------------------------------------------------------------

---------------------------------------------------------------

---------------------------------------------------------------

---------------------------------------------------------------

---------------------------------------------------------------

3. How does high animal protein consumption correlate with liver cancer in rats, and what are the implications for human health?

---------------------------------------------------------------

---------------------------------------------------------------

58

4. What are the negative effects of chemotherapy on the immune system and how does it potentially allow fungal infections to spread?

------------------------------------------------------------

------------------------------------------------------------

------------------------------------------------------------

------------------------------------------------------------

------------------------------------------------------------

------------------------------------------------------------

------------------------------------------------------------

------------------------------------------------------------

------------------------------------------------------------

------------------------------------------------------------

------------------------------------------------------------

------------------------------------------------------------

------------------------------------------------------------------------

------------------------------------------------------------------------

## Action Prompts

1. Research and learn more about the work of Dr. Tullio Simoncini and his use of sodium bicarbonate to treat cancer caused by fungus.

2. Explore the research of Dr. T. Colin Campbell and his findings on the impact of a low-protein or high plant protein diet on tumor growth.

3. Reflect on the effectiveness of current medical cancer treatments, such as chemotherapy, and consider alternative approaches.

4. Investigate the role of fungus in contributing to the development and progression of cancer.

5. Learn about the connection between an acidic environment and fungal growth, and how an alkaline environment can help prevent and treat fungal infections.

6. Explore the concept of an antifungal diet, which involves eliminating sugar and yeast from the diet and incorporating alkaline foods and herbs with antifungal properties.

7. Consider the importance of maintaining a proper pH balance in the body and learn about acid-forming and alkaline-forming foods.

8. Understand how certain types of fungi, like Candida, can release toxins and promote inflammation, contributing to the development of cancer.

9. Explore the factors that can influence the presence of fungus, such as hormonal changes, diet, and lifestyle habits.

10. Learn about the importance of maintaining a balanced pH level in the body, avoiding certain foods and substances, and incorporating alkaline-forming foods to prevent fungal growth and reduce the risk of cancer.

11. Reflect on the connection between fungal infections and the weakening of the immune system, creating an environment conducive to cancer growth.

12. Consider the role of a healthy diet and lifestyle in preventing fungal infections and reducing the risk of cancer.

13. Explore natural remedies and lifestyle changes that can support the body's ability to heal itself and address the root cause of fungal infections.

14. Reflect on the relationship between fungus and cancer and consider strategies to prevent and combat both conditions.

# CHAPTER 7 The Role Of Genes In Disease: Are We In Bondage To Defective Genes?

Chapter 7 of the book "Self Heal by Design" delves into the role of genes in disease and challenges the notion that we are bound by defective genes. The chapter begins by explaining the nature of genes and their role in determining the development and functioning of our bodies. While acknowledging that genetics do play a part in disease susceptibility, the author argues that they are not the sole determining factor.

The chapter explores the concept of genetic determinism and questions the idea that our genes are solely responsible for our health outcomes. It highlights the work of scientists and researchers who have challenged the traditional view of genetics, including the concept of pleomorphism, which suggests that microorganisms can adapt and change in response to their environment. This challenges the notion that genes are fixed and unchangeable.

Furthermore, the chapter emphasizes the significance of environmental factors, lifestyle choices, and the body's internal terrain in the development and progression of disease. It stresses that while genes may contribute to disease susceptibility, they are not the only factor at play. Proper nutrition, hydration, and emotional well-being are highlighted as crucial elements in maintaining a healthy internal environment and supporting the body's natural healing processes.

The chapter also discusses the impact of minerals on the human genome and how deficiencies in certain minerals can lead to DNA mutations. It addresses the influence of environmental toxins, such as chemicals and heavy metals, on DNA structure and function. The authors advocate for organic food and clean environments to prevent DNA damage.

Additionally, the concept of epigenetics is explored, which suggests that gene expression can be influenced by environmental factors. The chapter presents research that demonstrates the significant impact of conditions in the womb and early childhood on gene expression and long-term health outcomes.

The authors argue against toxic treatments like chemotherapy and radiation, asserting that they do not address the root causes of cancer and can be harmful to the body. They advocate for alternative treatments that work in harmony with the body's natural healing mechanisms.

In conclusion, Chapter 7 emphasizes that while genes may play a role in disease, they are not the sole determining factor. The chapter encourages readers to take control of their health outcomes through lifestyle choices and by creating a healthy internal environment. It emphasizes the need to address the underlying causes of disease rather than merely treating symptoms.

## Key Lessons

1. Genes are not the sole determining factor in disease development: While genes can play a role in disease susceptibility, they are not the only factor that determines our health outcomes. Environmental factors, lifestyle choices, and epigenetics also play a significant role in gene expression and disease development.

2. The importance of a holistic approach to health: The chapter emphasizes the importance of taking a holistic approach to health and understanding the interconnectedness of various factors. It encourages readers to focus on creating a healthy internal environment through proper nutrition, hydration, and lifestyle choices.

3. The role of minerals in the human genome: The chapter highlights the importance of minerals in the human genome and how deficiencies in minerals can lead to DNA mutations. It specifically mentions the role of minerals like selenium and iodine in stabilizing DNA and preventing mutations.

4. The concept of epigenetics: The chapter delves into the concept of epigenetics, which suggests that our environment and lifestyle choices can influence gene expression. It mentions studies that show how factors like nutrition, emotions, and social interactions can impact the expression of genes.

5. The power of proactive self-care: The chapter challenges the notion that we are helpless victims of our genes and empowers readers to take control of their health through proactive self-care. By addressing factors like nutrition, hydration, and lifestyle choices, the author suggests that we can influence the expression of our genes and potentially prevent or mitigate the impact of certain diseases.

## Reflection Questions

1. How does the concept of genetic determinism challenge the idea that we are bound by defective genes?

---------------------------------------------------------------

---------------------------------------------------------------

66

2. What role do lifestyle factors play in influencing gene expression and disease risk, according to the chapter?

---------------------------------------------------------------------

---------------------------------------------------------------------

---------------------------------------------------------------------

---------------------------------------------------------------------

---------------------------------------------------------------------

---------------------------------------------------------------------

---------------------------------------------------------------------

---------------------------------------------------------------------

---------------------------------------------------------------------

---------------------------------------------------------------------

---------------------------------------------------------------------

---------------------------------------------------------------------

--------------------------------------------------------------

--------------------------------------------------------------

3. How does the emerging field of epigenetics suggest that our genes are not fixed and can be influenced by environmental factors?

--------------------------------------------------------------

--------------------------------------------------------------

--------------------------------------------------------------

--------------------------------------------------------------

--------------------------------------------------------------

--------------------------------------------------------------

--------------------------------------------------------------

--------------------------------------------------------------

--------------------------------------------------------------

--------------------------------------------------------

--------------------------------------------------------

--------------------------------------------------------

--------------------------------------------------------

--------------------------------------------------------

--------------------------------------------------------

4. What potential impact can our choices and actions have on our gene expression and overall health, as discussed in the chapter?

--------------------------------------------------------

--------------------------------------------------------

--------------------------------------------------------

--------------------------------------------------------

--------------------------------------------------------

--------------------------------------------------------

--------------------------------------------------------

--------------------------------------------------------

--------------------------------------------------------

--------------------------------------------------------

--------------------------------------------------------

--------------------------------------------------------

--------------------------------------------------------

--------------------------------------------------------

--------------------------------------------------------

## Action Prompts

1. Reflect on your beliefs about the role of genes in disease. Do you believe that genes are solely responsible, or do you think other factors play a significant role?

2. Research the concept of pleomorphism and its implications for disease. How does this challenge the traditional belief in genetic determinism?

3. Explore the work of Dr. Tullio Simoncini and his use of sodium bicarbonate to treat cancer. What are your thoughts on this approach?

4. Investigate the findings of Dr. T. Colin Campbell regarding the relationship between protein consumption and cancer. How does this research contribute to the understanding of genetic influence on disease?

5. Consider the concept of epigenetics and how it suggests that gene expression can be influenced by environmental factors. How does this change your perspective on the role of genes in disease?

6. Evaluate the importance of nutrition and diet in relation to gene expression and disease prevention. How can you incorporate a balanced and nutrient-rich diet into your lifestyle?

7. Reflect on the idea that our lifestyle choices and environmental factors can influence our genetic expression. How does this empower you to take control of your health?

8. Consider the significance of a holistic approach to health, addressing both genetic and lifestyle factors. How can you incorporate exercise, stress management, and environmental awareness into your daily life?

9. Research the impact of minerals on DNA function and the role they play in disease development. How can you ensure you are getting the necessary minerals in your diet?

10. Reflect on the overall message of the chapter and how it challenges the belief in being bound by defective genes. How does

this change your perspective on your own health and genetic predispositions?

# **CHAPTER 8 Fuel For Life: Food Performs Or Deforms**

Chapter 8 of the book "Self Heal by Design" delves into the crucial role that food plays in maintaining optimal health and preventing disease. The author emphasizes that the food we consume can either fuel our bodies and promote well-being or contribute to the development of chronic illnesses.

The chapter begins by highlighting the significance of nutrition in supporting the body's natural healing processes. A well-balanced diet that includes whole foods, fruits, vegetables, and lean proteins is essential for maintaining a healthy body. On the other hand, the consumption of processed foods, refined sugars, and unhealthy fats can lead to inflammation and the onset of chronic diseases.

The author also explores the impact of food on the gut microbiome, which is vital for overall health. A diverse and balanced microbiome is crucial for proper digestion, nutrient absorption, and immune function. The chapter emphasizes the importance of consuming probiotic-rich foods and avoiding medications like antibiotics that can disrupt the balance of gut bacteria.

Furthermore, the chapter delves into the concept of food as medicine. The author discusses the healing properties of certain foods and herbs, emphasizing the benefits of incorporating anti-inflammatory foods, antioxidants, and immune-boosting ingredients into the diet. These elements support the body's natural healing processes.

In addition to general health, the chapter specifically addresses the prevention and treatment of diseases such as cancer and fungal infections. It explains how certain foods can contribute to the growth of fungus and yeast in the body. The chapter recommends eliminating sugars, yeast, and refined carbohydrates from the diet to starve the fungus. It also suggests incorporating antifungal foods and herbs like garlic, olive leaf extract, oregano oil, and grapefruit seed extract to combat the fungus.

The chapter further emphasizes the importance of maintaining an alkaline pH balance in the body to prevent the growth of fungus. It explains how an acidic environment can promote the multiplication of fungus and suggests consuming alkalizing foods such as green vegetables, green drinks, and green supplements to restore the pH balance.

Overall, Chapter 8 of "Self Heal by Design" provides a comprehensive guide on using food as a tool for maintaining a healthy body and preventing diseases. It emphasizes the importance of making conscious and informed choices about the foods we consume to promote optimal health and well-being.

## Key Lessons

The key lessons from Chapter 8 of "Self Heal by Design" are:

1. Food is the fuel that provides energy for our body's functions. The quality of the fuel we consume directly affects our health and vitality.

2. A balanced diet that includes a variety of nutrient-rich foods is essential for optimal functioning and overall well-being. This includes fruits, vegetables, whole grains, lean proteins, and healthy fats.

3. Processed foods can have negative effects on our health, as they are often high in unhealthy fats, sugars, and additives. These can contribute to inflammation, weight gain, and chronic diseases.

4. Staying hydrated and consuming an adequate amount of water throughout the day is crucial for maintaining optimal bodily functions and supporting overall health.

5. Mindful eating, which involves paying attention to the taste, texture, and satisfaction of the food we consume, can help us make healthier food choices and prevent overeating.

By following these principles, individuals can support their body's natural healing processes and promote overall well-being.

## Reflection Questions

1. How can I make more informed choices about the food I consume to support my body's functions and prevent disease?

---------------------------------------------------------------

---------------------------------------------------------------

---------------------------------------------------------------

---------------------------------------------------------------

---------------------------------------------------------------

---------------------------------------------------------------

---------------------------------------------------------------

---------------------------------------------------------------

---------------------------------------------------------------

---------------------------------------------------------------

---------------------------------------------------------------

---------------------------------------------------------------

---------------------------------------------------------------

---------------------------------------------------------------

---------------------------------------------------------------

2. What are some specific nutrient-dense foods that I can incorporate into my diet to ensure I am getting essential vitamins, minerals, and antioxidants?

---------------------------------------------------------------

---------------------------------------------------------------

3. How can I reduce my consumption of processed and unhealthy foods that can contribute to inflammation, weight gain, and chronic diseases?

-------------------------------------------------------------------

-------------------------------------------------------------------

-------------------------------------------------------------------

-------------------------------------------------------------------

-------------------------------------------------------------------

-------------------------------------------------------------------

-------------------------------------------------------------------

-------------------------------------------------------------------

-------------------------------------------------------------------

-------------------------------------------------------------------

-------------------------------------------------------------------

-------------------------------------------------------------------

------------------------------------------------

------------------------------------------------

4. What steps can I take to create a balanced and nutritious diet that can help prevent diseases like heart disease, diabetes, and certain types of cancer?

------------------------------------------------

------------------------------------------------

------------------------------------------------

------------------------------------------------

------------------------------------------------

------------------------------------------------

------------------------------------------------

------------------------------------------------

------------------------------------------------

------------------------------------------------

------------------------------------------------

------------------------------------------------

------------------------------------------------

------------------------------------------------

------------------------------------------------

## Action Prompts

1. Evaluate your current diet and identify any imbalances or deficiencies in essential nutrients.

2. Make a list of alkaline-forming foods and incorporate them into your meals to maintain a balanced pH level in your body.

3. Limit your consumption of acidic-forming foods to prevent the growth of fungus and yeast in your body.

4. Incorporate green vegetables and grasses into your diet to help cleanse and alkalize your body.

5. Consider the harmful effects of processed foods and prioritize consuming whole, natural foods.

6. Experiment with recipes using legumes such as black-eyed peas, red lentils, and chickpeas to add nutritious options to your meals.

7. Explore dressings and pates made from tahini, sunflower seeds, and linseed as healthy alternatives to processed condiments.

8. Take note of the lifestyle habits that contribute to maintaining the body's acid/alkaline balance, such as oxygen, sunshine, temperance, rest, exercise, water, salt, and mental health.

9. Seek practical tips on how to incorporate healthy eating habits into your daily life for long-term health benefits.

# CHAPTER 9 Conquering Candida- And Other Fungus/YeastRelated Problems

Chapter 9 of the book "Self Heal by Design" is titled "Conquering Candida- And Other Fungus/Yeast-Related Problems." In this chapter, the author provides a comprehensive overview of Candida overgrowth and other fungus/yeast-related problems in the body. The chapter emphasizes the importance of addressing the underlying causes of these issues and offers practical advice and strategies for addressing them naturally.

The author begins by explaining that Candida is a type of yeast that naturally exists in the human body but can cause health problems when it becomes overgrown due to a disruption in the body's natural balance. Factors such as a weakened immune system, poor diet, stress, and the use of antibiotics or other medications can contribute to Candida overgrowth.

The chapter highlights the importance of a holistic approach to treating Candida overgrowth, rather than just focusing on symptom management. The author recommends a three-pronged approach, which includes starving the fungus, killing the fungus, and restoring the balance of beneficial microbes in the body.

To starve the fungus, the author advises eliminating sugars and yeast from the diet. This includes avoiding cane and beet sugar, honey, fruits, fruit juices, yeasted bread, alcoholic beverages, yeast spreads, and yeast extracts. It is also important to avoid old food and grains that are susceptible to fungal growth.

The next step is to kill the fungus using various herbs and foods with antifungal properties. The author suggests incorporating herbs such as garlic, olive leaf extract, oregano oil, pau d'arco, horopito, and grapefruit seed extract into the diet or taking them in supplement form.

The final step is to restore the balance of beneficial microbes in the body, particularly in the gastrointestinal tract. This can be achieved by consuming probiotic supplements containing acidophilus and bifidus, as well as consuming fermented foods that promote the growth of healthy gut flora.

In addition to Candida overgrowth, the chapter briefly touches on other fungal and yeast-related problems, such as athlete's foot, ringworm, and fungal infections of the nails. The author suggests natural remedies and lifestyle changes to prevent and treat these conditions.

Overall, Chapter 9 provides a comprehensive overview of Candida overgrowth and other fungus/yeast-related problems, offering practical advice and strategies for addressing these issues naturally. The chapter emphasizes the importance of addressing the underlying causes and provides specific recommendations for dietary changes, supplementation, detoxification, and lifestyle modifications.

## Key Lessons

The key lessons from Chapter 9 of "Self Heal by Design" on conquering Candida and other fungus/yeast-related problems are:

1. Understanding Candida: The chapter explains what Candida is and how it can overgrow in the body, leading to various health problems.

2. Symptoms of Candida Overgrowth: It discusses the common symptoms of Candida overgrowth, such as fatigue, digestive issues, skin problems, and mood disorders.

3. Causes of Candida Overgrowth: The chapter explores the factors that contribute to Candida overgrowth, including a high-sugar diet, antibiotic use, hormonal imbalances, and a weakened immune system.

4. Dietary Changes: It emphasizes the importance of following an anti-Candida diet, which involves eliminating sugar, refined carbohydrates, and processed foods. The chapter also suggests incorporating more whole foods, vegetables, and probiotic-rich foods into the diet.

5. Natural Remedies: The chapter discusses various natural remedies that can help combat Candida overgrowth, such as herbal supplements, essential oils, and probiotics.

6. Lifestyle Changes: It highlights the significance of making lifestyle changes to support the body's ability to fight Candida, including stress management, regular exercise, and adequate sleep.

7. Detoxification: The chapter explains the importance of detoxifying the body to eliminate toxins and support the healing process. It suggests methods such as sauna therapy, colon cleansing, and liver support.

8. Seeking Professional Help: The chapter advises seeking guidance from healthcare professionals, such as naturopaths or functional medicine practitioners, who can provide personalized treatment plans and support.

Overall, Chapter 9 provides a comprehensive overview of Candida overgrowth and offers practical strategies for addressing this issue through dietary changes, natural remedies, lifestyle adjustments, and professional guidance.

## Reflection Questions

1. How can I incorporate more alkaline-forming foods into my diet to help prevent and address fungus/yeast-related problems?

-------------------------------------------------------------------

-------------------------------------------------------------------

-------------------------------------------------------------------

-------------------------------------------------------------------

86

---------------------------------------------------

---------------------------------------------------

---------------------------------------------------

---------------------------------------------------

---------------------------------------------------

---------------------------------------------------

---------------------------------------------------

---------------------------------------------------

---------------------------------------------------

---------------------------------------------------

---------------------------------------------------

2. What lifestyle habits can I adopt to maintain a balanced pH level in my body and inhibit fungal growth?

3. Are there any specific herbs or foods with antifungal properties that I can incorporate into my diet to help kill fungus?

----------------------------------------------------------------

----------------------------------------------------------------

----------------------------------------------------------------

----------------------------------------------------------------

----------------------------------------------------------------

----------------------------------------------------------------

----------------------------------------------------------------

----------------------------------------------------------------

----------------------------------------------------------------

----------------------------------------------------------------

----------------------------------------------------------------

----------------------------------------------------------------

------------------------------------------------

------------------------------------------------

4. How can I ensure that I am properly addressing and preventing Candida and other fungal infections in my body?

------------------------------------------------

------------------------------------------------

------------------------------------------------

------------------------------------------------

------------------------------------------------

------------------------------------------------

------------------------------------------------

------------------------------------------------

------------------------------------------------

------------------------------------------------

------------------------------------------------------------

------------------------------------------------------------

------------------------------------------------------------

------------------------------------------------------------

## Action Prompts

- Implement a sugar-free diet to starve the fungus and yeast.

- Incorporate probiotics into your daily routine to restore the balance of beneficial microbes in the gut.

- Seek professional guidance if necessary to address candida and other fungal/yeast-related problems.

- Avoid certain foods that can contribute to fungal overgrowth.

- Follow the specific diet plan provided in the chapter for conquering candida and other fungus/yeast-related problems.

# CHAPTER 10 Acid And Alkaline Balance: Precision Is Everything

Chapter 10 of the book "Self Heal by Design" delves into the significance of maintaining an acid and alkaline balance in the body. The author emphasizes the precision required to achieve this balance and how it can impact overall health and well-being.

The chapter begins by explaining that the body functions optimally when pH levels are balanced, with a slightly alkaline environment being ideal. However, various factors in modern lifestyles, such as stress, poor diet, and environmental toxins, can disrupt this balance and lead to an acidic state in the body.

The author provides detailed information on the effects of acidity on the body, including increased inflammation, weakened immune system, and impaired detoxification processes. They also highlight the role of acid-forming foods, such as processed foods, sugar, and animal products, in contributing to acidity.

To restore and maintain an alkaline state, the author recommends adopting a diet rich in alkaline-forming foods, such as fruits, vegetables, and whole grains. They also suggest incorporating alkaline supplements, such as green powders or alkaline water, into the daily routine.

The chapter emphasizes the importance of individualized approaches to achieving acid and alkaline balance, as everyone's body is unique. It encourages readers to listen to their bodies and make adjustments to their diet and lifestyle accordingly.

Furthermore, the chapter goes beyond the general importance of acid and alkaline balance and specifically focuses on the prevention of fungus and yeast-related problems. It explains that fungus thrives in an acidic environment and maintaining the correct pH balance is crucial for preventing the multiplication of these organisms.

The chapter provides information on the pH scale and how slight variations in pH can significantly impact the body's biochemical reactions. It also discusses the role of the lungs and kidneys in regulating blood pH and emphasizes the importance of testing pH levels in urine and saliva.

To combat fungus, the author recommends eliminating sugar, yeast, and other foods that feed fungus from the diet. They also suggest incorporating antifungal herbs and foods, such as garlic, olive leaf extract, oregano oil, and grapefruit seed extract, into the diet to help kill the fungus. Additionally, the chapter highlights the importance of restoring the balance of beneficial microbes in the gut by consuming probiotics and fermented foods.

The chapter concludes by reiterating the relationship between fungus and acidity, explaining that fungus creates an acidic condition in the body and thrives in an acidic environment. It emphasizes the importance of alkalizing the body to deter and kill fungus and recommends consuming alkaline-forming foods, particularly green vegetables.

Overall, Chapter 10 provides a comprehensive overview of the acid and alkaline balance in the body, its impact on overall health, and practical tips for maintaining this balance. It addresses the prevention of fungus and yeast-related problems, offering specific dietary recommendations and highlighting the importance of individualized approaches.

## Key Lessons

The key lessons from CHAPTER 10 Acid And Alkaline Balance: Precision Is Everything from the book "Self Heal by Design" are:

1. Maintaining an acid-alkaline balance in the body is crucial for preventing the growth of fungus and yeast-related problems.

2. Fungus thrives in an acidic environment, so it is important to maintain a proper pH balance for optimal health.

3. Slight deviations from the normal pH can have a significant impact on the body's biochemical reactions.

4. Avoiding foods that are high in sugar and yeast can help prevent the growth of fungus.

5. Incorporating alkaline-forming foods, such as green vegetables, into the diet can help alkalize the body and create an environment that is inhospitable to fungus.

6. Green drinks and supplements, like green barley or wheatgrass juice, can help alkalize the body and cleanse the tissues.

7. Factors like the return of periods after breastfeeding and consuming a large amount of figs can contribute to an acidic environment in the body, promoting fungal growth.

8. Maintaining an acid-alkaline balance can help prevent various health issues, including fungal infections and inflammation.

## Reflection Questions

1. How can I ensure that I am maintaining a balanced pH level in my body?

--------------------------------------------------------------

--------------------------------------------------------------

--------------------------------------------------------------

--------------------------------------------------------------

--------------------------------------------------------------

--------------------------------------------------------------

--------------------------------------------------------------

--------------------------------------------------------------

--------------------------------------------------------------

--------------------------------------------------------------

--------------------------------------------------------------

--------------------------------------------------------------

--------------------------------------------------------------

2. What are some specific dietary changes I can make to promote a more alkaline environment in my body?

------------------------------------------------

------------------------------------------------

------------------------------------------------

------------------------------------------------

------------------------------------------------

------------------------------------------------

------------------------------------------------

------------------------------------------------

------------------------------------------------

------------------------------------------------

------------------------------------------------

------------------------------------------------

----------------------------------------------------------------

----------------------------------------------------------------

3. How can I incorporate more alkaline-forming foods into my daily meals and snacks?

----------------------------------------------------------------

----------------------------------------------------------------

----------------------------------------------------------------

----------------------------------------------------------------

----------------------------------------------------------------

----------------------------------------------------------------

----------------------------------------------------------------

----------------------------------------------------------------

----------------------------------------------------------------

----------------------------------------------------------------

-----------------------------------------------------------------

-----------------------------------------------------------------

-----------------------------------------------------------------

-----------------------------------------------------------------

4. What lifestyle habits can I adopt to support optimal pH balance and overall health?

-----------------------------------------------------------------

-----------------------------------------------------------------

-----------------------------------------------------------------

-----------------------------------------------------------------

-----------------------------------------------------------------

-----------------------------------------------------------------

-----------------------------------------------------------------

-----------------------------------------------------------------

------------------------------------------------------

------------------------------------------------------

------------------------------------------------------

------------------------------------------------------

------------------------------------------------------

------------------------------------------------------

------------------------------------------------------

## Action Prompts

1. Evaluate your current acid-alkaline balance by monitoring your diet and lifestyle habits.

2. Increase your consumption of alkaline-forming foods, such as vegetables, to maintain a healthy pH balance.

3. Eliminate or reduce the intake of acid-forming foods, such as sugar, alcohol, caffeine, meat, and dairy products.

4. Incorporate antifungal herbs and foods into your diet to prevent fungal growth.

5. Follow the recommended 80% alkaline-forming foods and 20% acid-forming foods diet to maintain a pH balance of 6.5 in your cells.

6. Practice lifestyle habits that promote an acid-alkaline balance, such as getting enough oxygen, sunshine, rest, exercise, water, salt, and maintaining good mental health.

7. Consider incorporating a green drink recipe into your daily routine to alkalize your body.

8. Monitor your acid-alkaline balance regularly to ensure you are maintaining the desired levels.

9. Seek guidance from healthcare professionals or experts in maintaining an acid-alkaline balance for personalized advice and recommendations.

10. Educate yourself on the effects of an imbalance and the importance of precision in achieving and maintaining an acid-alkaline balance.

# CHAPTER 11 The Stomach's Secret Weapon: Hydrochloric Acid And Digestion

Chapter 11 of the book "Self Heal by Design" provides a comprehensive overview of the role of hydrochloric acid (HCl) in the stomach and its importance in digestion. The chapter begins by highlighting the significance of HCl in the digestive process. It explains that HCl is responsible for activating enzymes that break down proteins, stimulating the release of bile and pancreatic enzymes, and creating an acidic environment that kills bacteria and parasites.

The chapter delves into the process of HCl production in the stomach. It explains that HCl is produced by the parietal cells in the stomach lining and is released into the stomach when food is ingested. The production of HCl is regulated by various factors, including the presence of food, hormones, and nerve signals.

The chapter also discusses the importance of maintaining proper levels of HCl in the stomach. It explains that low levels of HCl can lead to poor digestion, nutrient deficiencies, and an increased risk of infections. On the other hand, excessive levels of HCl can cause acid reflux, heartburn, and other digestive issues.

To support HCl production in the stomach, the chapter provides several tips. It suggests eating a balanced diet that includes foods that stimulate HCl production, such as apple cider vinegar and lemon juice. It also recommends avoiding processed foods and managing stress, as these factors can affect HCl production.

Additionally, the chapter suggests considering supplementation with digestive enzymes or betaine HCl if necessary.

Overall, Chapter 11 of "Self Heal by Design" emphasizes the importance of hydrochloric acid in the stomach for digestion. It explains the role of HCl in breaking down food, killing harmful microorganisms, and maintaining optimal digestive health. The chapter provides practical tips for supporting HCl production and maintaining a healthy stomach environment.

## Key Lessons

1. Hydrochloric acid (HCl) is produced by the stomach and plays a crucial role in breaking down food and killing harmful bacteria and pathogens.

2. HCl helps activate enzymes, such as pepsin, which are responsible for breaking down proteins into smaller molecules.

3. Low stomach acid can lead to poor digestion, nutrient deficiencies, and an increased risk of infections.

4. Factors such as stress, aging, nutrient deficiencies, and certain medications can reduce HCl production in the stomach.

5. Symptoms of low HCl production include bloating, gas, heartburn, indigestion, and nutrient deficiencies.

6. There are various methods to test stomach acid levels, including the Heidelberg pH test and the baking soda test.

7. Certain dietary and lifestyle changes can help support HCl production, such as eating a balanced diet, managing stress, and avoiding certain medications.

## Reflection Questions

1. How well do I understand the role of hydrochloric acid in digestion and its importance in maintaining a healthy stomach?

-----------------------------------------------------------------

-----------------------------------------------------------------

-----------------------------------------------------------------

-----------------------------------------------------------------

-----------------------------------------------------------------

-----------------------------------------------------------------

-----------------------------------------------------------------

-----------------------------------------------------------------

-----------------------------------------------------------------

-----------------------------------------------------------------

------------------------------------------------------------

------------------------------------------------------------

------------------------------------------------------------

------------------------------------------------------------

2. Have I been mindful of my diet and lifestyle choices that can affect stomach acid levels?

------------------------------------------------------------

------------------------------------------------------------

------------------------------------------------------------

------------------------------------------------------------

------------------------------------------------------------

------------------------------------------------------------

------------------------------------------------------------

----------------------------------------------------------------

----------------------------------------------------------------

----------------------------------------------------------------

----------------------------------------------------------------

----------------------------------------------------------------

----------------------------------------------------------------

----------------------------------------------------------------

3. Have I experienced any symptoms that could be related to low stomach acid, such as poor digestion or nutrient deficiencies?

----------------------------------------------------------------

----------------------------------------------------------------

----------------------------------------------------------------

----------------------------------------------------------------

------------------------------------------------

------------------------------------------------

------------------------------------------------

------------------------------------------------

------------------------------------------------

------------------------------------------------

------------------------------------------------

------------------------------------------------

------------------------------------------------

------------------------------------------------

------------------------------------------------

4. What steps can I take to support the production of hydrochloric acid and optimize my digestion for better overall health?

## Action Prompts

1. Explore the role of hydrochloric acid in digestion and its importance in the stomach.

2. Discuss the function of hydrochloric acid in breaking down food and aiding in nutrient absorption.

3. Examine the effects of low stomach acid on digestion and nutrient absorption.

4. Investigate the potential causes and symptoms of low stomach acid.

5. Discuss the importance of maintaining optimal levels of hydrochloric acid for overall digestive health.

6. Explore natural ways to support and enhance stomach acid production.

7. Discuss the potential risks and benefits of using hydrochloric acid supplements for digestive health.

8. Examine the role of hydrochloric acid in preventing bacterial overgrowth in the stomach.

9. Discuss the potential link between low stomach acid and digestive disorders such as acid reflux and GERD.

10. Explore the impact of stress and lifestyle factors on stomach acid production and digestion.

# CHAPTER 12 Liver: The Project Manager

Chapter 12 of the book "Self Heal by Design" delves into the liver's role as the project manager of the body. The liver is responsible for a multitude of functions that are crucial for maintaining overall health and well-being.

The chapter begins by highlighting the liver's role in detoxifying the body. It constantly filters out toxins and waste products from the blood, converting them into less harmful substances that can be eliminated from the body. This detoxification process is essential for maintaining optimal health.

Additionally, the liver plays a vital role in digestion by producing bile. Bile aids in the breakdown and absorption of fats, ensuring proper digestion and nutrient absorption. The liver also regulates various metabolic processes, including the metabolism of nutrients, the storage of vitamins and minerals, and the production of important proteins and enzymes.

The author emphasizes the importance of supporting liver health through proper nutrition and lifestyle choices. A balanced diet rich in fruits, vegetables, and whole grains is recommended to provide the necessary nutrients for optimal liver function. Excessive alcohol consumption should be avoided, as it can be detrimental to liver health. Maintaining a healthy weight is also crucial for liver health.

The chapter also highlights the importance of regular exercise and stress management in promoting liver health. Exercise helps improve blood flow to the liver, aiding in its detoxification processes. Stress management techniques, such as meditation or deep breathing exercises, can also support liver health by reducing the impact of stress on the body.

Furthermore, the chapter provides practical advice on how to support liver function. This includes avoiding toxins and chemicals that can burden the liver, incorporating liver-supportive herbs and supplements, and ensuring proper hydration. The liver requires antioxidants, B vitamins, minerals, and herbs to effectively detoxify the body.

In summary, Chapter 12 of "Self Heal by Design" focuses on the liver's role as the project manager of the body. It emphasizes the liver's responsibilities in detoxification, digestion, and metabolic regulation. The chapter highlights the importance of maintaining a healthy liver through proper nutrition, lifestyle choices, regular exercise, and stress management. Practical tips are provided to support liver function, including avoiding toxins, incorporating liver-supportive herbs and supplements, and staying hydrated. Overall, the chapter provides a comprehensive overview of the liver's functions and the importance of maintaining its health for overall well-being.

## Key Lessons

1. The liver plays a crucial role in maintaining overall health and fighting disease. It acts as the body's project manager and master chemist, responsible for tasks such as detoxification, bile production, and nutrient storage.

2. Maintaining an alkaline pH balance in the body is important for preventing the growth of fungus and other harmful microorganisms. Fungus thrives in an acidic environment, so it is essential to maintain an alkaline pH to support overall health.

3. The liver has three phases of detoxification, and each phase requires specific nutrients and herbs for support. Antioxidants, B vitamins, minerals, and fatty acids are important for supporting liver function and detoxification.

4. The chapter provides a liver cleanse program and instructions for a castor oil compress to aid in liver detoxification. These methods can help support the liver's detoxification processes and promote overall health.

5. Legumes, such as black-eyed peas, red lentils, and chickpeas, are described as nutritious and alkalizing foods that can be beneficial for the liver. The chapter includes several recipes that incorporate legumes, providing practical ways to incorporate them into a healthy diet.

Overall, the key lessons from Chapter 12 of "Self Heal by Design" are the importance of the liver in maintaining overall health, the significance of maintaining an alkaline pH balance, the three phases of liver detoxification and the nutrients and herbs needed to support each phase, and the benefits of incorporating legumes into a healthy diet for liver health.

## Reflection Questions

1. How well do I understand the functions and importance of the liver in maintaining overall health?

-------------------------------------------------------------------

-------------------------------------------------------------------

-------------------------------------------------------------------

-------------------------------------------------------------------

------------------------------------------------

------------------------------------------------

------------------------------------------------

------------------------------------------------

------------------------------------------------

------------------------------------------------

------------------------------------------------

------------------------------------------------

------------------------------------------------

------------------------------------------------

2. Am I taking proper care of my liver through nutrition and lifestyle choices?

114

3. Do I understand the potential impact of fungus on liver health and the link between fungus and liver diseases?

------------------------------------------------------------

------------------------------------------------------------

------------------------------------------------------------

------------------------------------------------------------

------------------------------------------------------------

------------------------------------------------------------

------------------------------------------------------------

------------------------------------------------------------

------------------------------------------------------------

------------------------------------------------------------

------------------------------------------------------------

------------------------------------------------------------

--------------------------------------------------------------------

--------------------------------------------------------------------

4. Am I aware of the role of antioxidants, B vitamins, minerals, herbs, and fatty acids in supporting liver function, and am I incorporating these into my diet?

--------------------------------------------------------------------

--------------------------------------------------------------------

--------------------------------------------------------------------

--------------------------------------------------------------------

--------------------------------------------------------------------

--------------------------------------------------------------------

--------------------------------------------------------------------

--------------------------------------------------------------------

--------------------------------------------------------------------

---------------------------------------------------------------

---------------------------------------------------------------

---------------------------------------------------------------

---------------------------------------------------------------

---------------------------------------------------------------

---------------------------------------------------------------

## Action Prompts

1. Consume a balanced diet that supports liver health, including alkaline-forming foods.

2. Stay hydrated by drinking plenty of water throughout the day.

3. Avoid toxins such as alcohol, drugs, and processed foods that can negatively impact liver function.

4. Incorporate legumes into your diet, as they are a good source of protein and fiber and can help maintain a healthy pH balance in the body.

5. Try recipes that include legumes, such as lentil soup, chickpea curry, and black bean pate.

6. Take steps to detoxify and cleanse the liver, such as following a liver cleanse program or incorporating liver-supporting herbs into your diet.

7. Practice healthy lifestyle habits, such as regular exercise and stress management, to support overall liver health.

8. Consider consulting with a healthcare professional or nutritionist for personalized recommendations on supporting liver health.

# CHAPTER 13 Recipes

Chapter 13 of the book "Self Heal by Design" focuses on providing recipes that promote self-healing in the body. The chapter includes a variety of recipes that utilize natural, whole foods to support the body's healing processes. These recipes are designed to provide nourishment and support to the body, addressing various health concerns and promoting overall well-being.

The recipes in this chapter cover a range of categories, including breakfast, lunch, dinner, snacks, and desserts. Each recipe is made with ingredients that are known for their health benefits and healing properties. The author emphasizes the importance of using organic, fresh, and nutrient-dense ingredients to maximize the healing potential of the recipes.

Some examples of the recipes included in this chapter are the Healing Green Smoothie, which is packed with leafy greens, fruits, and superfoods like chia seeds and spirulina. This smoothie provides essential nutrients and antioxidants to support the body's healing processes. The Immune-Boosting Soup is made with ingredients like garlic, ginger, turmeric, and medicinal mushrooms, which help strengthen the immune system and fight off infections.

The Gut-Healing Salad includes fermented vegetables, avocado, and walnuts, which support gut health and promote a healthy digestive system. The Anti-Inflammatory Stir-Fry features ingredients like turmeric, ginger, and colorful vegetables, which help reduce inflammation in the body and support overall health. Lastly, the Healing Chocolate Avocado Mousse is a dessert made with avocado, cacao powder, and natural sweeteners like honey or maple syrup. It provides a rich and indulgent treat that is also packed with antioxidants and healthy fats.

Overall, the recipes in this chapter aim to provide nourishment and support to the body's natural healing processes. By incorporating these recipes into a balanced and healthy diet, individuals can support their overall health and well-being. The chapter also emphasizes the importance of alkaline-forming foods and includes recipes that help balance the body's pH levels. Additionally, legumes are highlighted in this chapter, with recipes featuring lentils, chickpeas, and beans. These recipes emphasize the nutritional benefits of legumes, which are high in protein, fiber, and essential nutrients. The chapter also provides tips and guidance on incorporating these recipes into a healthy lifestyle.

## Key Lessons

The key lessons from Chapter 13 of the book "Self Heal by Design" are:

1. The importance of eating a balanced diet: The chapter emphasizes the importance of eating a balanced diet to support the body's natural healing processes and maintain optimal health.

2. Incorporating legumes into a balanced diet: The chapter provides various recipes using legumes, such as lentils, chickpeas, and kidney beans, and offers instructions on how to prepare them for cooking. Legumes are a nutritious and flavorful option for incorporating into a balanced diet.

3. Plant-based salad dressing recipe: The chapter includes a recipe for a plant-based salad dressing that is suitable for vegetarian and vegan diets. The dressing is made with ingredients like

linseed/flaxseed, garlic, Celtic salt, maple syrup, lemon juice, basil, oregano, marjoram, and olive oil.

4. Barbara O'Neill's journey and philosophy: The chapter provides information about the author, Barbara O'Neill, and her journey into natural health. It highlights her belief in the body's ability to heal itself and her approach of working with the body to achieve healing responses.

Overall, the key lessons from Chapter 13 focus on the importance of a balanced diet, incorporating legumes into meals, and providing a plant-based salad dressing recipe.

## Reflection Questions

1. How often do I incorporate recipes into my meal planning and cooking routine?

---------------------------------------------------------------------

---------------------------------------------------------------------

---------------------------------------------------------------------

---------------------------------------------------------------------

---------------------------------------------------------------------

---------------------------------------------------------------------

----------------------------------------------------------------

----------------------------------------------------------------

----------------------------------------------------------------

----------------------------------------------------------------

----------------------------------------------------------------

----------------------------------------------------------------

----------------------------------------------------------------

----------------------------------------------------------------

----------------------------------------------------------------

2. What types of recipes do I typically gravitate towards and how can I expand my repertoire to include more diverse options?

----------------------------------------------------------------

----------------------------------------------------------------

123

124

3. How do I feel about experimenting with new ingredients and flavors in my cooking, such as incorporating legumes or trying out vegetarian or vegan-friendly recipes?

------------------------------------------------------------

------------------------------------------------------------

------------------------------------------------------------

------------------------------------------------------------

------------------------------------------------------------

------------------------------------------------------------

------------------------------------------------------------

------------------------------------------------------------

------------------------------------------------------------

------------------------------------------------------------

------------------------------------------------------------

------------------------------------------------------------

--------------------------------------------------------

--------------------------------------------------------

4. How can I make the process of meal preparation and cooking more enjoyable and fulfilling for myself?

--------------------------------------------------------

--------------------------------------------------------

--------------------------------------------------------

--------------------------------------------------------

--------------------------------------------------------

--------------------------------------------------------

--------------------------------------------------------

--------------------------------------------------------

--------------------------------------------------------

--------------------------------------------------------

--------------------------------------------------------

-------------------------------------------------------------------

-------------------------------------------------------------------

-------------------------------------------------------------------

-------------------------------------------------------------------

## Action Prompts

1. Incorporate alkaline-forming foods into your diet to promote a more alkaline pH in your body.

2. Try the "Great Green Drink" recipe to cleanse and alkalize your body on a daily basis.

3. Experiment with different legumes, such as black-eyed peas, red lentils, and chickpeas, in your meals.

4. Prepare and cook legumes using ingredients like onions, garlic, ginger, tomatoes, olive oil, herbs, and spices.

5. Explore different dressings and spreads, such as tahini mayo dressing, tahini dressing, sunflower seed pâté, and garlic linseed dream.

6. Follow the vegan recipe for a garlic and herb dressing using linseed/flaxseed, garlic, Celtic salt, maple syrup, lemon juice, basil, oregano, marjoram, and olive oil.

7. Store the garlic and herb dressing in the fridge for up to 5 days for future use.

8. Learn more about the author, Barbara O'Neill, and her background in natural health and healing.

Made in the USA
Las Vegas, NV
04 October 2023